From Hell to Heaven, Helped by Angels

A MINDFUL MAKEOVER THAT DRAWS YOU
FROM DESPAIR TO DELIGHT

NICHOLA WINTER

*This book is dedicated to Monica, whose love and
enthusiasm for angels is an inspiration.*

Contents

Free Gifts!

As a 'thank you' for buying my book I'd like to offer you **two** free gifts.

The first is an audio file (mp3 format) of the meditations. It can be hard to concentrate on meditating if you're having to read the words at the same time. With this gift you can simply close your eyes, relax and follow the meditation as it is read gently to you.

The second gift invites you to harness your inner child and get busy with your coloring pencils or crayons. Each of the angel illustrations is available to you as a printable download so that you can lose yourself in a world of imagination and therapeutic coloring.

To get your free gifts, just go to:

www.pilgrimsperch.com/angels-your-free-gifts/

I hope you enjoy your gifts. Have fun!

Acknowledgements

My gratitude goes to all who have helped this book come into being. Angels come in many guises, sometimes recognized and at other times unnoticed. Their inspiration is felt through the encouragement and support of many fellow pilgrims on the life journey and I thank them all:

Monica, my mother-in-law, who encouraged me from initial idea to end product; Ken Leeder, for interpreting my ideas and producing a perfect cover design; Polona Vovk, for the beautiful illustrations; Farah Canicosa for help with the layout and Christopher John Payne, for his guidance, imagination and constructive criticism.

I am thankful for the many angels who watched over me on the way.

Finally, heartfelt thanks to Nicholas, my husband, who was wise, patient and insightful throughout the whole process.

About the Author

 Nichola has spent the last 20 years as a priest helping people just like you handle the problems they face with the guidance of angels. An experienced retreat leader and spiritual guide, Nichola has overcome illness and obstacles in her own life with the help of angels and she has written this book to show the astonishing impact they can have in transforming your life.

Introduction

Introduction

You're struggling.

You feel pain.

It's like you're paralyzed. You can't move forward and get on with life.

You feel depressed, guilty and as though nothing on earth can possibly help.

In other words, life feels pretty much like hell at the moment.

Now is the time you need to be taken gently by the hand and offered understanding and compassion. Allow yourself to be shown a path that will take you away from the bad things you are experiencing.

Here's a foolproof method that will place you on a firmer footing, the first rung of a 'stairway to heaven.'

You can do this.

Angels can help.

Consider the following, written in the seventeenth century:

> *Angels were the first creatures God made,*
> *created pure as the light, ordained with the*
> *light to serve God, who is the Lord of Light.*
> *They have charge to conduct us, wisdom to*
> *instruct us and grace to preserve us. They*
> *are the Saints' tutors, Heaven's heralds,*
> *and the Bodies' and Souls' guardians…[1]*

Angels are found in many of the world's faith and belief traditions. In some they have names; in others they are anonymous or unidentified. But they all have something to offer us. They can help in many of life's difficult situations.

Angels are there for you. They come into our lives as compassionate, life-affirming messengers. What is the thing that angels are most often quoted as saying?

'Do not be afraid...'

Read on to discover just how you can move from hell to heaven, unlocking comfort, wisdom and compassion with the aid of angels.

Try it – you may like it. Discover a completely new way of living and dealing with all that life throws at you.

Where Are You Now?

Chapter 1

Where Are You Now?

Sometimes we just feel lost. Out of it. Not ourselves. Certainly not the person we feel we were formed to be. A very wise former Archbishop, the Rt Revd David Hope, once said:

"Religion isn't about being good; it is about being holy, and being holy has nothing to do with being pious. It has much more to do with becoming or being the person God created and wants us to be."

This is sound advice for every single one of us – no matter what faith path we may tread.

There are times when we find life is being really difficult. That's when we need to 'come home' to ourselves, to be at ease with ourselves and to know peace. It's not always easy to achieve that serene state. But help is at hand. If we allow ourselves to accept the aid that angels offer we'll discover a rich vein of golden wisdom that can deliver far more than we might have thought possible.

Basilian Father Thomas Rosica says:

"Angels are very important, because they provide people with an articulation of the conviction that God is intimately involved in human life."

That's an amazing statement. Can it really be that angels are so prepared to help us?

Let's consider what angels are. They are messengers from God – the deity in whom we live and move and have our being. Angels can help us become our real selves – the people that God wants us to be; fulfilling our potential; dealing with the issues that can make life so difficult at times. They can help us reclaim our gifts for the benefit not only of ourselves, but for those closest to us as well as the larger community, both local and worldwide. Remember, angels aren't just for Christmas, they are there for us all year round.

The poet Christina Rossetti wrote the following:

> *I go from earth to heaven*
>
> *A dim uncertain road,*
>
> *A houseless pilgrim through the world*
>
> *Unto a sure abode:*
>
> *While evermore an Angel*
>
> *Goes with me day and night,*
>
> *A ministering spirit*
>
> *From the land of light,*
>
> *My holy fellow-servant sent*
>
> *To guide my steps aright.*[1]

So how can we tap into the wisdom and help that angels bring?

We need to have a starting point. Reconnecting with your heart is a good way to do this. Life can be chaotic, difficult, challenging – or just plain busy

21

– and in order to move forwards we often need to stand still, take a deep breath, take stock and relax. Stilling ourselves, enabling ourselves to reconnect with our heart, that center of our being without which we cannot function at all, means we can then take the first steps to achieving our full potential.

So, how can you reconnect with your heart?

First of all, start with your current situation – which may well be a lot more positive than you may think. Consider your achievements, gifts, the good things in your life. It's a bit like counting your blessings. Name them, recognize them and enjoy them. Imagine talking to an angel about what is going on in your mind. Allow yourself to remember times when you have received praise or compliments. Don't feel guilty at 'self-indulgence' or dwell on what is sometimes called 'imposter syndrome', or 'perceived fraudulence'. These involve feelings of self-doubt and personal incompetence that persist despite your education, experience and accomplishments. Commentator Elizabeth Cox says:

> *"Once you're aware of the phenomenon,*
> *you can combat your own imposter*
> *syndrome by collecting and revisiting*
> *positive feedback.*[2]*"*

Listen carefully to words of encouragement, enjoy them and reflect on them – this can be invaluable in soothing your anxieties the next time self-doubt creeps in. Also, be assured that you're not alone. Talking about our fears with others can help us realize that other folk have the same fears – and very often any feelings of inadequacy are simply not valid.

Ok, so having overcome this hurdle, check in with how you're really feeling right now. Body scan practices can help us address just how we're feeling physically – and this is so often overlooked. Pockets of tension build up, pressures increase and we end up feeling tied up in knots. This does little to help us relax and live life to the fullest.

Body Scan Exercise

- Sit comfortably! If possible have your head, neck and spine aligned, your feet on the floor. Ideally, close your eyes…

- Become aware of your breathing. Is it fast, have you just sat down and it's a bit faster than usual? Just take a few seconds to be still and let your breathing return to a regular rhythm. Breathe in through your nose and out through your mouth. As you settle into a gentle rhythm, picture an angel sitting quietly at your side, breathing with you. Take a breath in and hold that breath for a few seconds. Imagine that you are breathing in cleansing, life-giving air – the oxygen we all need; then breathe out, ridding the body of stale air together with any worries, stresses or anxieties.

- Feel your body relax and slow down with each breath you take.

- Now focus on your feet; recognize how they connect with the ground. Be aware of each of your toes – those tiny digits so often overlooked and yet so important for helping us to find our balance as we stand, walk and move around.

- Move your focus up your legs to the knees. These joints are vital to our mobility – they help us stand tall, change direction and speed up or slow down.

- Gradually move your attention up to the abdomen. How are you sitting? Try to feel stable, safe and grounded.

- Now move your attention to the chest area. The ribcage provides a protective casing for lungs and heart. As you continue breathing be aware of the oxygen being pumped to your heart; essential fuel to keep it active, enabling you to live your own unique life.

- Let your thoughts move to your shoulders. Are they tense? Raised up and hunched? Let them relax; feel any tension drain out.

- Now think about your neck. Turn it very gently from left to right; move it up slightly so that the chin lifts; then down very gently. If you can, try some gentle circular motions, as though your nose is drawing a circle just in front of your face.

- Still that motion and let the focus move to your head. Be aware of your mouth – let it smile! Think about your nose – gently flare the nostrils and be aware of smells present around you. Next, concentrate on your ears – what do they hear? Be aware of sounds but don't let them impinge – just let them happen. Now to your eyes. Keeping your eyes closed gently roll your eyes and feel the delicate muscles that control your gaze.

- Move your attention to the top of your head – where a crown might sit (or a halo rest!) Let any tension dissolve. Imagine your angel massaging your temples, removing all stress and strain, clearing negative thoughts and allowing you to see clearly.

- Continue breathing gently for a few minutes, then slowly open your eyes.

- Visualize your angel sitting with you, welcoming you back as you realign yourself with your surroundings and your senses.

So now you're aware of how your body is feeling – calm and relaxed. Your breathing has become steady and your mind is stilled. What do we do next?

Read on.

The ANGEL Method

Chapter 2

The ANGEL Method

Having reconnected with your heart you should be feeling calm and relaxed but may now be wondering where we go from here. Time to engage the brain cells – and have some fun as well!

This is where you can let your imagination take flight as we explore the ANGEL Method; an exercise that will draw you from turmoil to blissful tranquility.

Take a blank sheet of paper – yes, real paper! – and a pen or pencil. On the left-hand side of the sheet form a column by writing in large lettering the following: A-N-G-E-L-S.

Beside each of the letters write a word, phrase or sentence describing your hope for the day ahead or an aspect where you feel you need help.

The following is an example but you can be as playful and creative as you want. Let your imagination run riot and fill in the spaces as you desire…

A is for Affirming

Each day brings a fresh start; it is a new day, bringing new opportunities, new horizons, new challenges. I shall embrace it, making the most of the special gifts only I have and rejoicing in being the person I am meant to be.

N is for New, Nourishing, Nurturing

Today begins with a new dawn; this day can nourish me, nurture and inspire me.

G is for Gift, Glorious, Glowing, Gentle, Grace

This day is a glorious gift, granted with grace and generosity. I can let go of guilt, grow in this new day and let its gentle and glorious touch glow in my encounters with others.

E is for Energized, Excited, Easy

I am excited about today. Some things will be easy; some things will be a challenge, but I can be energized and exhilarated about all the day will offer.

L is for Life affirming, Light

The light of this new day is life affirming. It brings a promise of new chances and new beginnings.

S is for Self-care, Salvation

The arrival of this day brings a pledge of nurture – I need to ensure I pay attention to self-care and the healing that it will bring.

Now you have a set of goals – a kind of 'wish list' of things you'd like angels to help you find. Not only does it include your needs but also it helps you recognize the good things in life and the gifts you bring to yourself and others. Check on the list throughout the day; review your progress (or lack of it). Don't despair if you find you haven't achieved everything on the first day. There's always tomorrow... Your list may change as days go by – some goals will happen easily; others may need more work. The angels are there to help you – and the next chapter explores how we can tap into their energy and wisdom.

Seven Angels to Help You Let Go

Chapter 3

Seven Angels to Help You Let Go

Angels may not be at our beck and call, but they are a constant presence in our world, ready to provide guidance when needed. With good meditation practice, an open heart and the right attitude, we can call upon their loving energy to help us and those around us to lead better, more fulfilling lives, both spiritually and practically.[1]

We need to remember that angels can't just be summoned at will. They can be invited into our life and, indeed, they will often appear unbidden. We need to be alive to possibilities – whether it be an encounter with another person, a piece of music, a work of art, a special place. By practicing meditation techniques we can increase the opportunities for encounters with those angels best suited to help us. The meditations in themselves are not quick-fix solutions but they can transport us into a frame of mind where we can deal with problems, fragile mind-sets and hard-to-face issues. Angels aren't magicians – they won't waft away problems with a sprinkle of fairy-dust. Angels are mediators and messengers between you and God; they will carry prayers and pleas for help to that source of all-being and they will deliver divine guidance in the form appropriate to your need. Angels will gently equip us with the tools we need; inspiration for prayer, meditation, mindfulness and practical processes that can help in all of life's complicated and complex situations.

Five Secrets for Letting Go of Demons

Don't allow demons to get you down! Demons can haunt us and lurk at the back of the mind or they can intimidate us and make us believe that they are in charge. But they're not. By adjusting our mindset and inviting the help of angels we can face down the demons and live a calmer, healthier and more fulfilled life.

So, how do we get rid of these demons?

- Be gentle with yourself. There's a saying – 'Rome wasn't built in a day' – and we need to build up our defenses gradually so we can banish those demons for good. It can take time and practice; we may take wrong turns and make mistakes but we don't have to beat ourselves up about it.

- Don't forget to breathe. The first and last thing we do in life is breathe. Breathing becomes second nature but we need to pay attention to how we breathe. Rapid, shallow breathing can cause anxiety and lack of concentration but a pattern of deep, regular breaths will slow you down and create a calmer mindset.

- Relax. Make yourself comfortable. Find a quiet, safe space away from risk of interruption. Sit or lie so that you can feel your limbs, muscles and mind becoming relaxed and free of tension.

- Focus. Find a way of meditating that works for you. Revisit Chapter One for some helpful hints. Light a candle and gaze at the flame, or place a flower in a small vase and focus on its shape, color and fragrance. Take time to wonder at its beauty.

- Slow down. Allow time for whichever of the following meditations you choose. Don't try to use too many at once. Meditation cannot be rushed – you need to slow down your body, brain and spirit in order to feel the full benefit of the exercise.

Seven Angels to Help You Fly Free

Now we're going to look at seven of the beloved archangels, their virtues and how they can help you take wing and fly. You may need to work through this section several times to become familiar with what each angel offers but don't be put off. Once you see how each angel offers help you'll be able to tap into their wisdom and include it in your life – each day and every day.

Michael

Michael is the Chief of the archangels, the head of the angelic army. His name, Michael, means 'who is as God'. He is a holy warrior and the Archangel of Protection.

Michael guards and strengthens us in battles against our own inner demons. He protects travellers and those who undertake difficult journeys. He can also be called on for emotional and psychic protection. The color associated with Michael is blue.

Mindful meditation: Setting ourselves free

The spiritual journey needs to begin free from baggage of pain, guilt, shame and blame. How do we cut those negative ties?

- Make yourself comfortable in a quiet place. Breath slowly and deeply, settling into a gentle regular pattern.

- Visualize the color blue. Picture blue skies, turquoise waters, the deep dark unending blue of the universe surrounding the planet we call home.

• Invite the archangel Michael to draw close. See him coming quietly to stand by your side.

• Imagine a large pack on your back. This is crammed full of things that are weighing you down.

- Ask Michael to take each of these items out. As he removes them, one by one, he holds them up for your inspection.

- Recognize and name them. Ask Michael to give you the courage and resolve to let them go.

- Imagine a large deep hole appearing in the ground. Allow Michael to cut the bag from your back and cast it into the hole, together with the contents.

- Watch attentively. Michael closes and locks the hole for all time. Nothing can escape and return to haunt you.

- Next, picture any people or issues holding you back. Imagine them connected to you with cords that restrict your freedom of movement.

- Visualize Michael's sword. It cuts through those cords, setting you free.

- Be thankful. Express gratitude to the Archangel Michael for his aid. Sit quietly and continue breathing; gradually bring your attention back to the present.

Gabriel

Gabriel is the Archangel of revelation; the bringer of truth, annunciation, guidance and resurrection. In the bible it was Gabriel who told the young girl, Mary, that she would give birth to Jesus, the

Messiah and Son of God. The name 'Gabriel' means 'God is my strength'. He provides guidance and direction for spiritual growth and is often depicted with a trumpet, illustrating his role as a messenger from God. Gabriel's associated color is white.

Mindful meditation: Guidance for the journey

For those who feel they lack direction in their lives Gabriel can provide guidance toward your true spiritual path and help you focus on setting goals and building a more fulfilling life.

- Sit comfortably in a quiet place. Close your eyes and breathe slowly and deeply. You may like to sit with the palms of your hands turned upwards in a gesture of receiving.

- Feel your body release tension as your breathing settles. Perhaps carry out the body scan exercise to check that you are completely relaxed.

- Random thoughts may enter your mind. Don't fight them but let them pass. Imagine them drifting away as you feel your focus turning towards Gabriel.

- Gabriel brings a pure white light. This re-energizing light of divine love, purifies mind, body and soul. White is the color that speaks of purity, of cleansing and truth. It is the color that is not a color and yet consists of all colors.

- Imagine yourself absorbing this light. It gently penetrates the crown of your head and flows to every part of your body.

- Ask Gabriel to guide you. Allow this light to bring clarity and direction as you continue your spiritual journey.

- Be aware of any thoughts, images or pictures that may form. Notice and register them but put them to one side for the present.

- Continue breathing. Allow Gabriel to withdraw but hold on to the light. Open your eyes and let your focus return to the here and now.

- Contemplate the thoughts that came to you. What might they be suggesting? Don't overthink things but return to them during the day, letting any inspiration and meaning gradually filter into your consciousness.

Raphael

Archangel Raphael is the healer and patron of travellers; one of the seven holy angels who attend the throne of God. The apocryphal text of Enoch describes him as 'set over all diseases and all the wounds of the children of men.' The name 'Raphael' means 'God has healed' or 'the shining one who heals'. For those intrigued by language 'Rapha' in Hebrew means 'healer' or 'doctor'.

Raphael can help with issues of healing, wholeness and integrity. He helps overcome disease, feelings of inadequacy and superstition; he can heal deep emotional wounds caused by breakdowns in personal relationships. Raphael guides us on our way and helps us find strength for the journey.

43

Meditation on Raphael can provide a channel for God's healing energy, whether on a personal, social or worldwide scale. Raphael's color is green, the color of nature and all living healing things. The healing that Raphael brings can be for yourself or it may be for others, be they present or at a distance.

Mindful meditation: Channeling healing energy

Focus on the person in need of healing. This might be yourself, or someone for whom you are concerned. Open your mind and heart to receive the energy of angels and envisage yourself acting as a channel for that energy to flow into the person you are thinking of.

- Sit comfortably and quietly in your meditation space. Close your eyes and breathe deeply. Be aware of any tension and deliberately let it go.

- Imagine a clear green light. It surrounds you, or the person you are thinking of.

- Feel yourself absorbing this light. Allow it to bring calming and soothing to any areas of pain, whether of body, mind or emotion.

- Empty your mind of all thoughts. Focus on the needs of yourself or the person in need of healing.

- In single words or short phrases name the pain that is affecting you.

- Visualize Raphael. He draws close to you and surrounds you with healing green light, the

color of nature and harmony. It might be a subdued, subtle green – the shade of sage or aspen leaves – or it may be a brilliant green, the dazzling pure green of costly emeralds. Allow the light to wrap around you, encircling you, holding you safely and restoring you to wholeness.

- Let words of thankfulness fill your mind. Offer them to Raphael, enabler and bringer of all healing.

- When you are ready open your eyes. Gently return to the day.

There can be great fellowship in joining 'prayer groups' praying for the whole of humanity at certain times of the day and you may like to use this meditation in thoughts and prayers for others and world situations.

Uriel

Uriel is the Archangel of salvation and ministration – he embodies angelic energy relating to purity of heart and true spiritual peace. His color is deep ruby red or purple.

In the book of Enoch Uriel is recognized as one of the four angels standing in the presence of God. The name 'Uriel' means fire, flame, light or sun of God.

Uriel can help us by bringing peace, enriching devotional worship and enabling service of others. He also helps us maintain the kind of detachment we need in order to keep things in perspective. Uriel helps us smooth out emotional turbulence in our lives, and gives us strength to remove feelings of selfishness and harmfulness.

In biblical traditions Uriel is the angel who stood at the gate of the Garden of Eden with the flaming sword.

Mindful meditation: Engaging with angels of peace

Uriel can bring tranquility of mind and enable each of us to be channels of peace. He can help release disturbing feelings or resentments you may be holding, whether towards yourself or others.

- Sit comfortably in your quiet space. Hold the palms of your hands in your lap, facing upwards, ready to receive.

- Imagine a deep red or purple light surrounding you. It is the color of a fine ruby wine or one of those stunning clear colors you can see in the sky at sunset.

- Concentrate on your breathing. Allow it to become regular and steady.

- Let any physical tension release.

- Focus on any areas of concern or negativity. Picture them drifting away in a bright, loving and warm light.

- Allow the words 'Peace, be still' to permeate your thoughts. Gradually focus on the single word 'Peace'.

- Identify those areas in your life where you need peace. Offer them to Uriel. Imagine him clasping them to his heart and transforming them with peace.

- Read or listen to the prayer of St Francis:

  Lord, make me an instrument of thy peace;

  where there is hatred let me sow love; where there is injury, pardon;

  where there is doubt, faith; where there is despair, hope;

where there is darkness, light; and where there is sadness, joy.

Lord, that I may seek to console rather than to be consoled;

to understand rather than to be understood;

to love rather than to be loved.

For it is in giving that we receive;

in self-forgetfulness that we find our true selves;

in forgiving that we are forgiven;

in dying that we are raised up to life everlasting.

- Remain sitting quietly. Immerse yourself in the peace that Uriel brings, before gradually returning to the day.

Chamuel

Chamuel is the Archangel of pure unconditional love. His name means 'He who sees God' and he witnesses to divine love and justice.

Artists often depict Chamuel with green wings, wearing armor and red tunic. The color linked to him is pink – a universal color associated with love. His qualities are love, tolerance and gratitude. He expresses a strong and supportive love which is unconditional, without any sense of control or

49

expectation of return. Chamuel helps restore lost self-esteem and heals the wounded heart. He enables you to find love, compassion, creativity and beauty in the people around you as well as in the surrounding environment.

Like Gabriel, Chamuel was believed to be one of the angels present in the Garden of Gethsemane at the agony of Christ, bringing strength and power to endure what couldn't be avoided. He also attended Jesus at the resurrection.

Chamuel encourages us to widen our capacity to love, to value working with the best possible intentions, for the benefit of all and not just ourselves.

Mindful meditation: Visualizing angelic love

Real love is strong and supportive; above all it is grounded in self-love; it is loving a person without needing to control them, allowing them to be free; it is nurturing without smothering; it is being true to your soul. [2]

In learning compassion and tolerance to ourselves and others Chamuel helps us to accept ourselves fully – we can then move on to projecting this love to others.

This meditation helps when self-esteem is low or if you are being too harsh on yourself, allowing negative energy to take over your life.

- Light a candle. Be comfortable in your quiet space.

- Imagine a warm non-judgmental pink light. It enfolds you and holds you safely.

- Breathe gently and steadily. Allow your body to relax.

- Imagine Chamuel drawing close. Allow his gentle light and warmth to fill your body and mind.

- Be aware of any areas the light does not reach. Ask Chamuel to permeate and fill them with his loving light.

- Think about any feelings of low esteem, negativity or resentment. See them dissolving and being replaced with compassion, forgiveness, tolerance and gratitude.

- Your heart is now filled with light. Like a flower unfurling its petals in the sun allow yourself to be completely open to Chamuel's glorious light. That light can be with you for all time. Carry it with you and allow it to shine in times of need.

Jophiel

The Archangel Jophiel is an angel of knowledge and wisdom, combining these gifts with the benefits of creativity, insight and spiritual enlightenment. These have traditionally been thought of as feminine gifts so Jophiel is often portrayed as being female.

'Jophiel' means 'beauty of God' and this angel is associated with art and beauty. Jophiel is the patron of artists. Meditating with Jophiel can bring wisdom, perception, clarity and insight. She can help in overcoming ignorance, pride, mental confusion and narrow-mindedness. As guardian of beauty and purity tradition has it that Jophiel was the angel who drove Adam and Eve from the Garden of Eden after they disobeyed God. Jophiel's color is yellow – the color of cornfields, flowers and bright noon sunglow, or the gentle hazy yellow of the moon's halo and distant stars that shine out at night.

Mindful meditation: Seeking clarity and insight

Meditation with Jophiel aims to help clear the mind of clutter; to open up new sources of knowledge and to bring enlightenment and inspiration. She helps us develop clear thinking, deeper understanding and foresight, and she fires up our creative intuition. This exercise can help if we feel we are confused or lacking in knowledge; it helps dissipate negativity and 'foggy thinking'.

- Sit comfortably in your quiet space. You may wish to light a candle.

- Breathe gently and steadily. Allow your body to relax but hold your back straight.

- Imagine you are surrounded by a clear yellow light. Breathe in that light, feel it tracking down through arms and legs until your body brims over with yellow radiance.

53

- Let the light swirl around you. Feel it gently embrace you in a soft golden mist.

- Imagine a spark of light in your heart. It grows into a ray of the light that beams upwards from the crown of your head. It reaches out to the creator of the universe, the source of all light and being.

- Jophiel is by you. Imagine asking her for help; for the blessings of creativity, understanding and clear thought.

- For what are you seeking guidance? Picture those issues and gently hold them up to Jophiel.

- Be still. Allow Jophiel's inspiration and aid to surround and sustain you. Remain held in that loving clasp as long as you need.

- When you are ready allow the light to dwindle. It becomes a thin strand – a bit like a thread of spider's silk – almost imperceptible but stronger than you can imagine. That lifeline of help will always be there to help when you need it.

- Continue breathing steadily. Slowly return to the present moment.

Zadkiel

Zadkiel is the Archangel of joy. His color is violet and he is often depicted with a violet flame representing the transformative power of joy. This can help release any negativity that is weighing you down and bring you to a more positive frame of mind.

The name 'Zadkiel' means 'the righteousness of God' and some religious writings portray Zadkiel as the archangel of benevolence, mercy and memory. Jophiel and Zadkiel are the two chieftains assisting Michael. They carry his standard and follow him directly into battle.

Some writings claim it was Zadkiel who prevented Abraham from killing his son Isaac as a sacrifice to God – Zadkiel is often depicted as holding a dagger. He can help with the transition from negative to positive energy. He also enables us to overcome feelings of entrapment, intolerance and hardness of heart.

Mindful meditation: Visualising transformation

Zadkiel's gift of bringing joy can help us rediscover the inner child – that innocent untouched being that each of us once was. Regaining that internal joy can help us recover our zest and enthusiasm for life. It provides a return to the balance that enables us to live life in all its fullness.

- Sit comfortably in your quiet space. Hold your back straight, your feet grounded on the floor.

- Breathe slowly and deeply. Feel your body settle in an alert but relaxed state.

- Picture the color violet. Delicate pansies, calming lavender or the warming violet you see in the golden flames of a glowing, cheering fire.

- Imagine standing up. Calmly and unhurriedly you step into a circle of violet flame.

- Feel the violet flames on the soles of your feet. They warm but do not burn you. Feel that warmth rise up through your whole body.

- Gradually let go of any feelings of negativity. Zadkiel helps you take them and hold them in the flames, where they dissolve and vanish.

- Feel purification from the flames. Breathe in Zadkiel's strength and let every outward breath release you from anything holding you back.

- Focus on your heart. Release painful memories or thoughts; allow scars to heal.

- Now focus on your mouth and throat. Imagine the flames gently erasing hurtful or unkind words.

- Sense the flames rising to your head. Gradually they enfold your thought processes and enable you to see and realize all that is good in yourself and in others.

- Feel yourself immersed in the joy of the angels. Imagine dancing with them, embracing their childlike freedom and spontaneity.

- Allow the flames to fade. However, you will still feel their beneficial effect.

- Open your mind to gratitude. Feel it flow through and over you as you return to the present and the events of the day.

Mantras: Singing With Angels

Chapter 4

Mantras: Singing With Angels

Here's the bad news. Meditations take time. We saw at the beginning of the last chapter that meditations in themselves are not quick-fix solutions. It takes practice and perseverance to become familiar with the techniques used but once we get the hang of them they are hugely helpful in bringing about a change in our approach to life. They help us to hope and they help us to cope. However, sometimes you may not have the luxury of time to spend on a lengthy meditation. So what about some good news?

Welcome to **mantras**. It's well known that these can transform our mental state and increase our feelings of well-being. Drawn from Hindu and Buddhist traditions, mantras were often used as teaching methods to aid concentration, meditation and prayer. They usually consist of a word or simple phrase repeated gently and quietly. The repetitive rhythm creates a steady, calming mindset that brings a sense of tranquility and peace.

Feelings of negativity, stress and anxiety are pushed back. Positive, hopeful and kindly feelings come into view. A new energy moves you forward. You find yourself singing in your mind. Singing with the angels.

The American singer/songwriter Snatum Kaur has written:

> *When we chant these mantras, the vibrations become a reality within our beings and within our experience...*

Chanting them can reduce stress levels, but yogis say it's doing much more than that: it's actually changing your brain's chemistry. The tapping of the tongue on the roof of the mouth sends messages and vibrations to areas of your brain and work with the brain and then the whole body to effect very, very real change.[1]

Vanessa Pawlowski, a psychologist based in Beverly Hills, says:

You're doing a mini-meditation when you're saying a mantra... It gives us something we can hold on to… There's a lot of negative self-talk, people getting stuck in judgment and playing the same thing over and over again [in their minds]. So I have them use mantras as a way of interrupting those negative experiences and instead give them something positive to focus on:

I'm going to love myself no matter what today.

Nothing can stop me today – I can only stop myself.[2]

You might think it amazing that something so simple can have such an astonishing and positive effect. What's not to like? So how can we create mantras from what we've learned about angels?

Here's how. We've seen how different angels can help in different situations. Imagine using a mantra inspired by your chosen angel. As you become more familiar with the meditation techniques and use different mantras you'll find yourself drawing comfort, reassurance and strength. Indeed, you may also find yourself creating your own mantras to help you tap into the help and energy of the angels you've read about.

Let's look at some situations and see how a helpful mantra might appear.

Do Not Be Afraid

Whenever anxiety or fear grips us we need to remember that we're not facing this alone. In the Bible, the Archangel Gabriel brought a startling message to the young girl Mary. He told her that she would give birth to a baby who would become the savior of the world. How scary and astonishing must that have been? But he tells her, "Do not be afraid". Mary trusts – she believes that she doesn't need to be afraid. She says 'yes' to the angel. 'Yes' to a seemingly impossible task – but Mary carries it through. So often, when we are faced with something that seems completely outside our ability, strength or imagination, we are given the resources to deal with it.

Gabriel is the bringer of truth and guidance. He helps build self-confidence. His name means 'God is my strength'. What mantra might we draw from Gabriel's wisdom? Try:

"Today I can be perfect"

"I do not need to be afraid"

Jordan Younger, from California, food blogger and founder of The Balanced Blonde, has written:

> *Two of my biggest weaknesses in achieving*
> *utmost peace and harmony with myself is*
> *fretting about the future and worrying*
> *about the past. Reminding myself*
> *that today, every day, I am in control of*
> *how I feel and the state of being I choose is*
> *very powerful to me.*[3]

How can you regain that feeling of being in control, of being confident and excited about the future? Perfection can be a tough goal – but every day is a new day. Each day brings new opportunities to try again. We've seen how the Archangel Gabriel says, 'Do not be afraid…' So often angels bring this message in their encounters with human beings.

The story of Daniel in the Bible (Daniel 6:16-23) tells how an angel protected him when he was cast into the lions' den. Daniel goes on to carry out more dangerous and apparently impossible tasks but angels are on hand to save and encourage him. Invariably their message is along the lines of "Do not fear, greatly beloved, you are safe. Be strong. Be courageous".

Again, when the angels come to the shepherds on the hillside to tell of the birth of Jesus, (Luke 2:8-11) the shepherds are, understandably, terrified at this sudden vision. But yet again the message is, "Do not be afraid". The angels are bringing a message of hope and good news.

The ninth century Greek monk St Joseph wrote:

> *Gabriel, the light of God, brings peace.*

You might adopt this as a mantra for yourself, inviting Gabriel's light to surround you with peace and a sense of well-being:

> **"Gabriel, light of God, bring me peace"**

Put simply:

> **"Do not be afraid"**

For Enduring Tough Times

The American Tibetan Buddhist, Pema Chodron, often uses this quote with her students:

> *You are the sky. Everything else is just the weather.*[4]

The sky represents truth; the weather suggests emotions. Clouds will gather, rain will fall and storms may come. But wait a little while and the sun will shine again. It's often said that the darkest moment comes right before the dawn. It can be hard to exercise patience and remember that the bad things will pass. We always want the good times to be right now!

In the book of Psalms we're given the message, "No evil shall befall you… he will command his angels to guard you" (Psalm 91:10-11). When we're longing for the clouds to clear and the sun to shine again our mantra can become:

"Evil shall not befall me. Angels will guard me"

Think back to the meditation with Michael; we saw how he takes the things that weigh us down, enables us to set them aside and banish their malign effect. You might want to use this mantra:

"Michael, help me let go"

If we feel in particular need of support we can think of the story about Jesus in the garden just before his death. The Gospel of Luke tells us, "an angel from heaven appeared to him and gave him strength" (Luke 22:43). Some traditions suggest that this was the Archangel Michael. We might use this mantra:

"Michael, bring me strength to endure;

help me see this task through"

For Expressing Gratitude

Gratitude is something we can all see in life if we look carefully – for small things as well as greater things. It's good to be mindful of these things and to be able to express thanks and appreciation for them.

Rachelle Tratt, founder of The Neshama Project in California, has written this:

> *Lately I have been playing with mantras as they relate to what I am looking to cultivate. Whatever it is that you may be looking to create in your life, state it in the present tense as if it's happening now: 'I am healthy'; 'I am strong'; 'I am open to receiving abundance in all forms.' Notice when you say the mantra out loud: Does it feel light? Does it ground you and make you feel good? If yes, then there it is!*[5]

We've considered how angels can help us with problems – but it's good to acknowledge our angels when things are going well too. Appreciating the good things in life creates a positive mindset; it prepares and strengthens us for the tough times. Plants that receive nothing but water often grow weak and spindly. A little bit of stress can be good – it helps us build up muscles to deal with problems. When you go to the gym you test yourself with weights and resistance to build strength and stamina. When problems in life assail us we can learn to deal with them by using mantras. That experience builds our confidence and helps us cope with other challenges as they arise.

Dag Hammarskjold, former Swedish peacemaker and Secretary-General of the United Nations, once said:

> *For everything that has been, thank you.*
> *For all that is to come, Yes!*[6]

If we rest on our laurels, taking the good things in life for granted, there's a danger that we become self-centered, lazy and over-expectant. Instead, we need to identify and express gratitude. In the biblical book of Job we hear how "the morning stars sang together and all the heavenly beings shouted for joy" (Job 38:7). The angels praise and give thanks to God – and so can we. Here is one of the classic prayers of thanksgiving from the Anglican Church:

> *With angels and archangels, and with all*
> *the company of heaven, we proclaim your*
> *great and glorious name, for ever praising*
> *you and saying: Holy, holy, holy Lord, God*
> *of power and might, heaven and earth are*
> *full of your glory. Hosanna in the highest.*[7]

It is an acknowledgement that everything that is good in life comes from God. We might make a mantra from this prayer:

> *"With the help of angels my life can be full of glory. Thank you"*

Recognizing that glory and expressing our thanks and gratitude can do much to bring about a sense of calm and well-being. We can do this by using the 'counting blessings' routine – something we'll look at in the next chapter on journaling.

Love for Myself and for Others

> *"Love bears all things, believes all things, hopes all things, endures all things"*

This beautiful phrase comes from the Bible (I Corinthians 13) – a passage often called 'The Hymn of Love'. It is frequently read at weddings and funerals. It's worth looking at the whole of the chapter – it contains some gems that you may like to use, such as:

> *"If I speak in the tongues of angels but do not have love I am nothing"*

> *"Love is patient; love is kind"*

> *"And now faith, hope and love abide, these three; and the greatest of these is love"*

We've seen how the angel Chamuel can teach us love and tolerance for ourselves and others. The meditation showed us how to envisage surrounding ourselves (or someone else) and being enfolded in unconditional love. You may like to use the following:

"May light and love surround me"

or, if you are thinking of another person or situation:

"May light and love fill/surround xxx"

Silent, Calm and Still

Sometimes just being still can be the hardest thing. Making space and time to be quiet, emptying the mind of all it's 'busy-ness' is a challenge in our time-impoverished lives. Uriel is the angel who brings peace and purity of heart. Making ourselves still and attentive is crucial if we want to hear, listen and understand without lots of external interference and interruption. Finding stillness is one of the keys to mindful engagement with the world. Only when we rest in that stillness can we perceive what and who is around us. We'll find angels in more places than we might think. We need to be aware and alert. The Very Revd James Atwell wrote a beautiful prayer containing these words:

*Creation is luminous with your love. All
things are your messengers. Unveil our
senses to perceive you, tune our spiritual
ears, give us eyes of the soul.*[8]

Allowing ourselves to be alert, aware and
conscious of possibility means that we can meet
angels in so many circumstances. We can be alive to
all things that might be messengers from God – and
then we can allow their peace and tranquility to
color and calm our lives. You might take one of the
phrases to form your own mantra, for example:

> **"Unveil my senses; tune my ears; give
> me eyes to see clearly"**

In the meditation with Uriel in Chapter 3 we used
the words, 'Peace, be still'. Write these words down
and then repeat them several times, removing one
word after a number of repetitions. Your piece of
paper will look like this:

Peace, be still.

Peace, be.

Still.

Feel the angel surrounding you with peace and
compassion. Repeat each line several times. Sense
the peace and stillness.

Comfort in Distress

Raphael is the angel of healing. Some traditions believe it was Raphael who stirred up the water of the pool of Bethesda, bringing healing to those who were dipped into it. It was Raphael who healed Jacob's hip after he wrestled with God in the wilderness. Words attributed to St Joseph the Hymnographer:

> *Raphael, God's cure, sends comfort in distress.*

From this we might create a mantra such as:

> **"Raphael, God's cure, bring me comfort"**

or

> **"Raphael, may God's cure dispel my distress"**

We need to remember that we don't always get the answers, help and relief straightaway – or in the form we expect! It was Julian of Norwich, the fourteenth century mystic, who wrote:

> *God did not say "You will not be tempest-tossed" but "You will not be overcome."*[9]

The problems, fears and difficulties we encounter in life may not always be 'magicked' away but, with the help of the angels, we'll be given the resources to find a way through.

73

Clarity of Thought

It doesn't have to be a crisis that makes you turn to angels for help.

Sometimes we need a boost for our concentration, for clarification of the mind, for dispelling 'fuzziness' of thought. We might have an exam, important meeting or tricky presentation coming up. We need to know that we are doing all we can to be as sharp and focused as possible. This is the time to turn to Jophiel – that wise angel of illumination. Jophiel can help us de-clutter the mind so that we can engage with the task in hand, embracing clarity and insight so we can address the problem and find the best way through.

> *"Jophiel, bring me light; bring me clarity; bring me wisdom"*

Angels are on Your Side

This might not strictly be a mantra but it is a truth we must never forget. The Bible provides many instances where God is on your side:

> *The angel of the Lord encamps around those who fear him, and he delivers them*
>
> *– Psalm 34:7*

and

> *I am sending an angel ahead of you to guard you along the way and to bring you to the place I have prepared*
>
> *– Exodus 23:20*

From these you can make mantras such as:

"May angels guard me this day. May angels guard me this way"

Compassion and tolerance towards others are key to forgiveness – for both yourself and for others. There is a phrase in the bible where we're told, "there is joy in the presence of the angels of God over one sinner who repents" (Luke 15:10). Angels want love to succeed; they want us to be at peace with those around us and they want us to engage with the world in a positive way. To 'repent' means to turn our thinking around, to be sorry for what has gone before and to look forward to taking a better path. That will make the angels rejoice. We'll feel pretty good about it as well!

The Joy of Angels

Angels help us express gratitude and they also help us identify and embrace joy in our lives. We all go through bad times but life well lived can be fulfilling and abundant with joy. You'll recall that we thought earlier about the priest who said that

75

we all have the capacity to become holy – and being holy doesn't mean being pious but 'becoming or being the person God created and wants us to be'. Once we achieve that state we can surely be joyful.

Zadkiel is the Archangel of joy – look back to the exercise with him in Ch3 – but all the angels express joy at creation and help us live the life we are formed for. Angels encourage us to rediscover that spontaneity that comes from a childlike delight in all that is around us, in all that helps us find our place in the world.

In the Bible we're told how Jesus stresses the importance of children when he says, 'their angels see the face of my Father in heaven'(Matt 18:10). He says, 'unless you change and become like children, you will never enter the kingdom of heaven' (Matt 18:5). From this we can see how the concept of guardian angels arose, an idea that has brought comfort and peace to many. The Bible refers to them as 'ministering spirits sent to serve those who will inherit salvation' (Heb 1:14).

When angels tell the shepherds of the birth of Jesus it is news of great and amazing joy. You sense their excitement and delight as they sing, 'Glory to God in the highest heaven, and on earth peace among those whom he favors' (Luke 2:14). God wants joy and peace for all his children. His angels come to bring us that message. We can repeat that message in a mantra expressing the joy we share with angels:

"Glory to God; peace to all people"

A Wealth of Mantras

There's a lot of material here and a lot of ideas for using mantras. You'll be able to pick out some favorites for different situations. You'll see how using shortened phrases from poems, hymns and prayers provides a rich abundance for creating our own mantras. It's helpful to keep a notebook for jotting down thoughts and inspirations as they occur. Why not develop this idea and create a scrapbook of these ideas with pictures – your own drawings or images from books, magazines, the internet? Angels can take so many forms and disguises – enjoy discovering them! It won't all happen overnight but you will find and build your own collection of mantras.

Three Angelic Experiences

In the meantime you might like to reflect on the following three angelic experiences that will inspire and encourage you to take control of your life. They remind us that we do not journey through life alone or purely in our own strength. That life force 'in whom we live and move and have our being' is there for us and sends angels as messengers to strengthen us. See these simple and straightforward phrases as a kind of 'emergency kitbag' of mantras that can help you when the going gets tough:

"Do not be afraid"

"The angel of God goes with me this day"

"Glory to God and peace to all people"

The Angeling of My Rest

Chapter 5

The Angeling of My Rest

You've come to the end of the day. Much has happened – some great, some not so great. What you need now is a good night's sleep. Sleep is absolutely crucial to our wellbeing. Too much and we become sluggish throughout the day. Too little and concentration, focus and creativity go out of the window.

So how do we ensure our sleep is refreshing, restoring and re-enabling?

This part of the book is called 'The Angeling of My Rest'. It finds its origins in the Celtic Christian tradition. Other faith patterns use similar techniques. The tips offered here are simple, practical and relaxing. They'll bring peace, they'll help quieten your mind and they'll enable you to unload the issues of the day. Together they'll combine to help you wind down at the end of the day and get that much needed rest and sleep that your body, mind and brain all need.

The PILLOW Exercise

This is where you can use what I call the PILLOW Exercise:

Pause

Invite

Linger

Let

Own

Whisper, wait and weight

Pause

First of all, *pause*. Find your quiet space. Focus on your breathing – gentle and regular. Imagine all the angels who have helped you during the day gathering around you, quietly and calmly; watching over you and holding you gently as you approach your time of rest.

Invite

Now, *invite*. This is the time to reflect on the words of 'The Angeling of my Rest' – also known as 'A Rest Benediction'. It goes like this:

Bless to me, O God, the moon that is above me,

Bless to me, O God, the earth that is beneath me,

Bless to me, O God, my wife and my children,

And bless, O God, myself who have care of them;

Bless to me my wife and my children,

And bless, O God, myself who have care of them.

Bless, O God, the thing on which mine eye doth rest,

Bless, O God, the thing on which my hope doth rest,

Bless, O God, my reason and my purpose,

Bless, O bless Thou them, Thou God of life;

Bless, O God, my reason and my purpose,

Bless, bless Thou them, Thou God of life.

Bless to me the bed companion of my love,

Bless to me the handling of my hands,

Bless, O bless Thou to me, O God, the fencing of my defense,

83

And bless, O bless to me the angeling of my rest;

Bless, O bless Thou to me, O God, the fencing of my defense,

And bless, O bless to me the angeling of my rest.[1]

The rhythm and down-to-earth quality of the prayer demonstrates a connection with the practicalities of every day life. 'Angeling of Rest' suggests entrusting our time of sleep to loving angels who will guard us through the night.

Formal prayers and invocations can seem a bit restrictive. You may want to adapt the wording or change the emphasis. The important thing is that you find something that works for you, that brings a gift from one or more of your angels and that brings you a sense of protection, calm and peace. The evening 'Journaling' exercise that we'll be using later can help with this. Bring the issues, problems and gifts of the day into your 'Angeling' prayer. Include them in what you are entrusting to the angels and allow them to be surrounded with love and guardianship.

Linger

Next, *linger*. Many of us will recall childhood bedtime prayers when we would pray that angels guard, keep and bless us through the nighttime hours and bring us safely to the new day. You may remember some of them:

> *May Michael be at my right,*
>
> *Gabriel at my left,*
>
> *Uriel behind me,*

Raphael before me –

and above my head,

the Presence of the Lord.[2]

The love and affection of the angels be to you.

The love and affection of the saints be to you.

The love and affection of heaven be to you,

To guard you and to cherish you.[3]

Shrine of the Soul

O God, give commandment to thy blessed angels

to make compassing of this steading tonight,

a company devoted, mighty and steadfast

to keep this shrine of the soul from harm;

Safeguard, O God, this household tonight,

its persons, its means of life, its good name,

delivering it from death, from danger, from harm,

and from the harvest of envy and hatred;

And, O God of peace, do thou grant us thankfulness with any loss,

that we obey thy laws below and enjoy thyself in the beyond,

where thou reignest for ever and ever. Amen.[4]

Let

L stands for *let* – as in *let yourself loose.*

Now think about writing down some of the stuff that's gone on during the day. Nobody else need read what's written here – it's just for you. Loosen your thoughts and really let yourself go... Journaling helps the mind unload all the 'stuff' at the end of the day. Good stuff you can enjoy, reflect on, give yourself a pat on the back. Less good stuff you can describe – don't flinch or shy away from writing the bad stuff down. Simply writing it down on paper really helps. The physical act of writing – forming words and sentences can point to a way through the tangle. You'll find yourself solving difficulties and problems before you know where you are. Or you'll be able to identify problems and uncover the right questions to ask so you can get help...

There are so many ways of journaling – but at the end of the day you'll be weary and you'll want to keep it simple. Invest in a good quality notebook you can write your thoughts in. You don't have to use a rigid format – but here are some ideas that you can 'mix and match' to suit your mood.

Reflection Journal

A reflection journal does just that. It reflects back to you events of the day, people you've met, how you've been feeling – both mentally and physically. You can record where angels have helped you. The journal can help you understand why such-and-such happened, why you reacted in a particular way, how you might have acted differently if you'd had the chance.

As your journal grows you'll be able to look back on what's happened before and see how you've progressed. It lets you monitor goals and good habits you may be trying to establish. Allowing yourself to be honest with yourself in your journal can provide insights that encourage you to change.

In order to reflect back on events, describe the event in as much detail as you can recall. What happened? How did you react? How did you feel? What might you have done differently? What can you learn from the event? Did angels help you with these events?

You may wish to include a 'to-do' list for tomorrow – a good way of decluttering the mind and preparing it for sleep, knowing that tomorrow is another day and there is always scope for improvement.

One Line a Day Journaling

Maybe you're really tired and your head just wants to hit that pillow – but if you can manage to write just one line a day that can help you pinpoint areas you want to pay more attention to. Writing just a single line can help you hold on to a memory – and even notice patterns when you look back that identify bits of your life crying out for attention.

This technique doesn't demand that you describe everything in detail. Key moments, brief sentences that capture the essence of an event – even if it seems rather mundane – will provide a memory for you to savor or material for you to think about on another occasion

One line a day journaling means you can do it relatively quickly. It won't overwhelm you but it will help you capture the moment and get into the habit of writing every day. You might like to think along the lines of:

- what was the best thing that happened to me today?

- what can I be thankful for from today's events?

- what was the biggest challenge from today?

- what is my biggest task or goal for tomorrow?

Gratitude Journaling

Keeping a gratitude journal where you write down everything you're thankful for is a kind of 'count your blessings' exercise. Studies have shown it can be used to banish depression, enrich relationships and give your self-confidence a boost. It will also lower stress and bring you calm as nighttime approaches. One of the most important things is that a gratitude journal can remind us to stop always striving for more and instead to just appreciate the present – which has so much to offer.

It's best if this exercise isn't rushed. Take a moment of quiet, be still and allow your mind to relive events of the day. Describe what you're thankful for; recall how it made you feel. Which angels helped you with this – and how? You may want to focus on one or two blessings rather than create an entire list. But enjoy the memory. Value the good things that have happened. You may want to write in depth about individuals, both past and present, who have had a good influence on your life.

You don't have to write the gratitude journal every day – once or twice a week works well. Here are some ideas you might like to use:

- write about a person from the past who influenced or helped you a lot

- write about an opportunity you had today

- jot down something good that happened unexpectedly during the day or earlier in the week

- describe something simple that brings you joy or peace of mind

Worst Case Scenario Journaling

This may seem counterintuitive but it was Mark Twain who once said:

> *I am an old man and have known a great many troubles, but most of them never happened.*[5]

Few of us can get through life without a variety of fears, worries and anxieties. And so many of them never come to fruition. But it doesn't stop us from worrying...

Here's what to do. Journaling about the worst-case scenario makes you confront your fears and then you find that many of your anxieties are irrational. Write about the worst that could happen, figure out just how likely that scenario actually is, how you'd react and handle it – and you'll probably find that things aren't nearly as bad as you'd imagined.

Later on you can look back on previous entries and see how rarely your nightmare fears actually occurred. Simply writing about these issues can help you understand the scenario – and even see a way through. A kind of grasping the nettle. (If you've ever tried that you'll know that taking a firm grip of a nettle doesn't cause pain but just brushing it or trying to hold it gently is when it causes the sting!)

Worst-case scenario journaling can help in identifying those negative thought patterns like catastrophic thinking (dwelling on irrational worst-case outcomes) or over-generalization ("things never work out for me"). Writing about your strengths and coping strategies will help you discover that you have much more in your personal armor than you think. Question what it is that you're really worried about. Write down your fears and doubts. Then ask yourself, "Okay, if that happens, then what?" and keep on asking yourself that question until your anxieties die down. The following sequence can help:

- define and describe your fear

- list how the worst-case scenario might be prevented

- list ways you might repair any damage

- write down the benefits of an attempt or partial success

- describe what might happen if you do nothing at all

These powerful journaling techniques enable us to name many of our demons. Once named and once shared with our angels (see Chapter 3) we'll find coping strategies that free us up to live our lives joyfully. We'll be using our gifts and talents fully and becoming the person we're meant to be.

Own

You've already done the hardest work. Now it's time to *own* the day and let it rest. All the events, the feelings, the emotions – they all happened to you, they were experienced by you and they brought you varying degrees of pain, joy, sadness and hope. *Own* them – don't deny them but don't let them take you over. Lay down your cares. A time for rest and sleep approaches and you need it to be as therapeutic as possible.

Whisper, Wait and Weight

Whisper 'good night' to the day and its events. Let the angels take it from here. *Wait* on the angels, let them take the *weight* of the day and whatever is lying on your mind. Let their gentleness and protection surround you as you lay down to sleep.

Pillow Fight

I hope the pillow exercise you've just done helps you drift off. Don't forget that the physical pillow you use is important too. Some like a soft pillow; some prefer something firmer. The Bible tells the story of Jacob journeying through the wilderness and coming to a place where he stays for the night. You can read about it in Genesis 28:10-22. Jacob picks a stone for a pillow. That night he dreams that he sees a ladder between earth and heaven. Angels ascend and descend the ladder. Imagine the scene – a dark night, wind blowing, stars overhead and the sound of jackals in the distance. Jacob feels fear and exhaustion… but eventually falls into sleep. See the angels as Jacob sees them; going up and down the ladder. Visualize them taking away the negative things that are causing you pain. Then visualize them bringing down from heaven, that place of blessing and sanctuary, things of peace, tranquility and calm… Remain restful. I hope your pillow won't be a stone – but don't fight it. Let your body relax and sink into slumber, blessed by angels.

Still can't get to sleep?

If you're still having difficulty calming down,
switching off or getting into the right mindset for
sleep here are some practical tips you can follow....

Make a helpful bedtime drink. Probably not alcohol! Warm milky drinks or herbal teas can calm and soothe.

Listen to some gentle relaxing music or sounds that provide beneficial calming…

Put away that phone, tablet or other electronic device. You're supposed to be switching off not switching on!

Repeat quietly to yourself one of the prayers we thought about earlier. Or a mantra that you have made up on your own. Counting sheep isn't always the failsafe it's claimed to be! Count angels instead…

Closing Thoughts

Chapter 6

Closing Thoughts

You were struggling.

You were in pain.

You felt as though you couldn't see a way forward and life was feeling a bit like hell itself.

You've come a long way since then…

You've probably found the path challenging but I hope you've found the exercises and techniques helpful. Connecting with angels who are just waiting to greet and help you can transform your life and enable you to view the world and your own situation with hope, optimism and joy.

So where do you go now?

The angels are always there. You can tune into them whenever you want to. They may not respond immediately but persevere. The more you practice the easier it will become.

Continue using the meditations. Calming the mind and stilling your thoughts helps prevent you from jumping to conclusions or making rash decisions. It was TS Eliot who wrote, 'In a minute there is time for decisions and revisions which a minute will reverse.' The first reaction may not always be the wisest...

Look out for material to create your own mantras. Find rhythms and patterns of words that keep angels influencing and blessing your life. Be creative. Be imaginative. Be playful and bold!

> *Promise fills the sky with light,*
>
> *Stars and angels dance in flight[1]*

Keep your eyes open – and your senses tuned. You never know where or when you might encounter an angel... or when you might be an angel for someone else. Life offers so many unexpected opportunities for us to be angels for others. We may not set out at the beginning of the day with that intention but encounters and situations may well cause us to be the right person in the right place for somebody in their time of need. Be alert and be aware. The writer of the letter to the Hebrews in the Bible says:

> *"Do not neglect to show hospitality to strangers, for thereby some have entertained angels unawares."*
>
> *– Hebrews 13:2*

I hope you've enjoyed reading this book and exploring some of the techniques described. It may well be that you have your own experience of angels – if you'd like to share it I'd love to hear from you. You can email me at:

nicky@pilgrimsperch.com

Remember, angels are on your side. We've seen how angels act as messengers, bringing compassion and affirmation into our lives. They help us become the people we're meant to be, and that is surely a joy.

Enjoy your journey of discovery with angels. May your encounters with angels be blessed – and may you be a blessing to others.

With every good wish,

Appendix: What Next?

There are lots of ways in which you can find out more about angels. Here are some ideas:

Biblical sources for further reading

- Abraham is prevented from killing his son by Zadkiel: Genesis 22

- An angel appears to Joseph: Matthew 1:18-25

- Angels tell the shepherds not to be afraid: Luke 2:8-11

- Daniel in the lions' den: Daniel 6:16-23

- Gabriel visits Mary: Luke 1:26-38

- Garden of Eden: Genesis 3:22-24 Jophiel (although not mentioned by name.)

- Garden of Gethsemane: Luke 22:43-46 An angel strengthens Jesus

- Hymn of Love: 1 Corinthians 13

- Joseph warned to flee into Egypt: Matthew 2:13-23

- Michael the Archangel: The Revelation to John 12:7-9

- Raphael: Book of Tobit, Apocrypha

- Story of Jacob wrestling with God: Genesis 28:10-22

- Story of Pool at Bethesda: John 5:2-9

- Uriel: Book of Enoch, ancient Hebrew apocalyptic text

Other Reading

- Astell, Christine, *Discovering Angels*, (2005) London, Duncan Baird Publishers Ltd. The Books of Enoch, Joseph B Lumpkin, (2009) Blountsville, Fifth Estate

- Davidson, Gustav, *A Dictionary of Angels*, (1967) New York, Simon & Shuster

- Langenberg, Ruth, *Angels: From Rosetti to Klee*, (2012) Prestel

- Grubb, Nancy, *Angels in Art*, (1995) Abbeville Press Inc, US

Other activities

- If you've enjoyed the free gift of coloring sheets there are many coloring books featuring angels available. Two examples are:

Hess, Lydia, *Sacred Angels: Coloring Experiences for the Mystical and Magical*, (2016) New York, Harper Collins

and

Happy Pandas Publishing (author*),Coloring Book with Angels,* (2021). Independently published and available at Amazon.

- If you'd like to find out more about forms of Christian worship and perhaps visit a church for a service see the website http://www.achurchnearyou.com for churches in the UK, or http://www.churchfinder.com for churches in the USA.

- Enjoy investigating poems and prayers featuring angels. Perhaps you can remember bedtime prayers you learned as a child – their simplicity conceals hidden nuggets of wisdom and makes them ideal for children from 1 to 99!

- Invest in a good quality book or diary for journaling – there's a fantastic selection around either in-store or online. Have fun choosing one that's right for you.

References

Introduction

1. Thomas Heywood, *The Hierarchy of the Blessed Angels*, 1635, available at http://archive.org.

Chapter One

1. Rosetti, Christina G, *To the End*, Poetry Foundation

2. Cox, Elizabeth, *What is imposter syndrome and how can you combat it?* Accessed 28th July 2021. http://mindful.org

Chapter Three

1. Astell, Christine, *Discovering Angels*, (2005) London, Duncan Baird Publishers Ltd.

2. ibid.

Chapter Four

1. Majewski, Lori, *Nine Empowering Mantras to shift your Mindset.* Accessed 9th September 2021. http://sonima.com

2. ibid

3. ibid

4. Chodron, Pema, *Meditation Quote 58*. Accessed 31st January 2022. http://dailymeditate.com

5. Tratt, Rachelle, *Nine Empowering Mantras to shift your Mindset.* Accessed 9th September 2021. http://sonima.com

6. Hammarskjold, Dag, *Top 25 Quotes by Dag Hammarskjold*. Accessed 9th November 2021 https://www.azquotes.com/author/6178-Dag_Hammarskjold

7. From Eucharistic Prayer, The Archbishops' Council (2000) *Common Worship*. London, Church House Publishing.

8. Atwell, The Very Revd. James, (2004) *At the Gate of Heaven*. Suffolk, St Edmundsbury Cathedral

9. Julian of Norwich, *Quotes.* Accessed 15th January 2022. http://goodreads.com

Chapter Five

1. Alexander Carmichael, (1992) *Carmina Gadelica*, Edinburgh, Floris Books.

2. Hopler, Whitney *Jewish Guardian Angel Prayers*. Accessed 20th January 2022.

http://learnreligions.com

3. Ed: de Waal, Esther, (1990) *The Celtic Vision*, Missouri, Liguori Publications.

4. McLean, GRD, (2008) *Prayers of the Western Highlanders*, London, SPCK.

5. Twain, Mark *Quotable Quotes*. Accessed 15th January 2022. https://goodreads.com

Summary

1. Vaughan Williams, Ursula, extract from libretto, *Hodie: A Christmas Cantata*, (1954) London, EMI Records.

One Last Thing...

I would really appreciate it if you would review my book on Amazon. Did it help you? What did you like about it? Were there things that could have been better? Did I miss anything that you'd have liked to have seen included?

You can drop me a line or ask me questions by emailing me at:

nicky@pilgrimsperch.com

Index

113